Awakening Your Inner Excellence: Mastering Your Mind for a Fulfilling Life

James Wonder

Published by Cecilia Agyemang, 2023.

While every precaution has been taken in the preparation of this book, the publisher assumes no responsibility for errors or omissions, or for damages resulting from the use of the information contained herein.

AWAKENING YOUR INNER EXCELLENCE: MASTERING YOUR MIND FOR A FULFILLING LIFE

First edition. August 12, 2023.

Copyright © 2023 James Wonder.

ISBN: 979-8223860129

Written by James Wonder.

Table of Contents

.... 1

Introduction 4

Chapter 1 7

Recognizing and Surmounting Restrictive Beliefs 8

Chapter 2 12

Nurturing a Mindset of Progress 13

Chapter 3 17

Harnessing Inner Resilience and Determination 18

Chapter 4 21

Illuminating Purpose and Igniting Passion 22

Chapter 5 26

Crafting a Vision for Your Life: Blueprint for Achievement 27

Chapter 6 31

Navigating the Path of Meaningful Goal Setting and Achievement 32

Chapter 7 36

Nurturing Your Well-Being and Growth in Today's Fast-Paced World 37

Chapter 8 41

Nurturing Positivity and Growth Mindsets for a Flourishing Life 42

Chapter 9 47

Weaving Bonds of Connection and Camaraderie 48

Chapter 10.. 53

Triumphing Over Trials with Unyielding Spirit and Determination 54

Chapter 11.. 58

Embracing a Mindset for Achieving Success.. 59

Chapter 12.. 63

Embracing Change and Taking Bold Action for Personal Growth.. 64

CONCLUSION 67

Awakening Your Inner Excellence

Mastering Your Mind for a Fulfilling Life

James Wonder

COPYRIGHT

Copyright (c) 2023 James Wonder

All rights reserved. No part of this publication may be reproduced, stored in a retrieval system, or transmitted in any form or by any means, electronic, mechanical, photocopying, recording, scanning, or otherwise, without the prior written permission of the copyright owner. The information contained in this book is provided for educational purposes only and is not intended as a substitute for professional medical advice, diagnosis, or treatment. The author and publisher make no representations or warranties with respect to the accuracy or completeness of the contents of this book and specifically disclaim any implied warranties of merchantability or fitness for a particular purpose. The author and publisher shall not be liable for any loss or damage caused or alleged to be caused directly or indirectly by the information contained in this book.

DISCLAIMER

The information contained in this book is not intended as a substitute for professional medical advice, diagnosis, or treatment. The author and publisher make no representation or warranties with respect to the accuracy, applicability, fitness, or completeness of the contents of this book. The information contained in this book is strictly for educational purposes. The reader assumes full responsibility for any actions taken based on the information contained in this book and the author and publisher shall not be held liable for any errors, omissions, or damages arising from its use.

Introduction

Meet Juanita, a successful businesswoman in her mid-30s. Juanita had achieved remarkable success in her career and was esteemed as one of the most adept and diligent employees in her company. However, despite her accomplishments, Juanita experienced a sense of emptiness and discontent in her life. She frequently found herself contemplating whether there existed a more profound purpose beyond her work.

One fortuitous day, Juanita stumbled upon a book titled " Awakening Your Inner Excellence: Mastering Your Mind for a Fulfilling Life " Intrigued by the title, Juanita made the decision to read this book.

As she delved further into the pages, she recognized that she had been constraining her own potential by subscribing to the notion that her career solely determined her success and contentment. She learned that she held the ability to shape the life she yearned for by shifting her perspective and tapping into her internal reservoir of strength.

Through the narrative of the book, Juanita discovered how to detect and surmount self-imposed limitations, cultivate a mindset of growth, and access her inner reservoir of strength to unleash her complete capabilities. Additionally, she unearthed practical methodologies to attain success and satisfaction across multiple facets of her life, including personal growth, relationships, and her professional journey.

Inspired by the insights she gained, Juanita embarked on integrating the techniques and strategies outlined in the book. She began prioritizing self-nurturing and personal advancement, fostering constructive habits, and setting objectives aligned with her values and aspirations.

Consequently, she commenced encountering an entirely new sense of fulfillment and joy in her life. Juanita discerned that by harnessing the potential of her mind and unleashing her inherent greatness, she could realize her utmost potential.

If you find yourself akin to Juanita, grappling with feelings of unfulfillment or dissatisfaction in your life, "Awakening Your Inner Excellence: Mastering Your Mind for a Fulfilling Life" could be the resource you require to transform your perspective and unlock your complete potential.

This book is meticulously crafted to guide you in tapping into your complete potential and fulfilling your aspirations by harnessing the power of your mind. Many individuals inadvertently restrict themselves by embracing the notion that they lack the capacity to realize their objectives or live the life they aspire to. Yet, the objective of this book is to dispel this constraining belief by equipping you with tools and methodologies to nurture a mindset that empowers you to achieve magnificence.

Within the pages of this book, you will gain insights into recognizing and conquering self-imposed barriers, fostering a mindset of growth, and accessing your internal reservoir of strength to unleash your untapped potential. Moreover, you will learn how to nurture habits and approaches that will propel you toward triumph in various spheres of your life, spanning personal development, relationships, and your professional journey.

Whether you are striving to enrich your well-being, prosperity, or joy, this book will furnish you with pragmatic and efficacious strategies to help you unlock your innate greatness and lead your most fulfilling life. So, if you are prepared to revolutionize your perspective and unleash your complete potential, let's embark on the journey presented by " Awakening Your Inner Excellence: Mastering Your Mind for a Fulfilling Life"

Chapter 1

Recognizing and Surmounting Restrictive Beliefs

Limiting beliefs serve as formidable barriers on the path toward embracing your innate potential and manifesting your most satisfying existence. These beliefs, characterized by pessimistic thoughts or perspectives, hinder our journey to full realization, often stemming from prior experiences or societal influences. Rooted deeply within our subconscious, these notions can deter us from embarking on ventures, pursuing aspirations, or embracing joy and contentment.

A pivotal approach to identifying limiting beliefs entails examining the pessimistic self-dialogue that we consistently engage in. For instance, you might catch yourself ruminating, "I lack adequacy," "Success isn't meant for me," or "My goals are unattainable." These cynical thoughts typically originate from limiting beliefs and can erode our self-esteem and self-assurance.

Another strategy involves discerning patterns. Limiting beliefs frequently manifest as recurrent behaviors. For instance, if you consistently shy away from novel experiences, it might signify a constraint in your belief concerning your capabilities.

Another valuable step involves seeking external feedback. Occasionally, attaining an external perspective proves beneficial. Request feedback from a dependable friend or mentor to identify any limiting beliefs that might be evident in your conduct.

To transcend limiting beliefs, the foremost step is cultivating self-awareness. A method to achieve this involves challenging our adverse thoughts and beliefs by scrutinizing their validity. Often, we discover that these unfavorable thoughts are rooted in assumptions or past occurrences that might no longer be pertinent or accurate.

To illustrate this process, consider the narrative of Kate. Kate had always harbored aspirations of initiating her own business venture. Yet, she confined herself due to the belief that she lacked the intellect and talent requisite for success. This belief stemmed from a past event in high school where a math test failure led her teacher to assert that business wasn't her domain. Despite her subsequent achievements, Kate clung to this limiting belief. When she eventually recognized its hindrance, she dismantled it by recalling her past triumphs and recognizing her worth. A mentor aided her in pinpointing her strengths and devising a strategy to establish her own business. Empowered with newfound assurance and direction, Kate surged past her limiting beliefs, establishing a prosperous consulting enterprise that brought her fulfillment and delight.

An alternate approach to surmounting these beliefs entails restructuring them from a positive angle. Shifting the focus from our deficiencies to our capabilities can be transformative. As an example, if you bear a belief that you are inadequate for pursuing your ideal vocation, you can reshape it by recalling your unique talents and strengths that could propel you toward excellence.

Enter the tale of John, a case in point. John had long nurtured a dream of becoming a professional athlete. However, he curtailed this dream due to the conviction that he lacked inherent athleticism. This notion emanated from an instance in his youth where he was excluded from his school's basketball team. Notwithstanding his inclination for running and zeal for fitness, John clung to this belief.

As he acknowledged its restrictive nature, he redirected his attention to his strengths and accomplishments. Engaging in marathon training and surrounding himself with supportive companions and mentors, he charted a course of accomplishment and gratification as a successful endurance athlete.

An additional potent means of dismantling limiting beliefs is action. By taking concrete steps toward your objectives, you substantiate your capacity and disprove the accuracy of these constraints.

Immersing Yourself in Positivity: Surrounding yourself with optimistic individuals, literature, and resources can aid in your quest to conquer limiting beliefs. Seek out role models who have realized what you aspire to accomplish and glean wisdom from their journey.

Nurturing Self-Compassion: As you navigate the endeavor to transcend limiting beliefs, practicing self-compassion proves pivotal. This process can be arduous, and setbacks are inevitable. Bestow upon yourself kindness and understanding as you traverse this odyssey.

Identifying and conquering limiting beliefs is an ongoing expedition. As you continue to evolve, new constrictions may emerge. However, armed with the right mindset and strategies, you possess the capability to surmount these barriers and access your innate magnificence.

To encapsulate, recognizing and surmounting limiting beliefs is a vital stride in the quest to unchain your inner greatness and actualize your most rewarding life. By cultivating awareness regarding negative thoughts and beliefs, challenging them, and reimagining them through a positive lens, you have the ability to liberate yourself from the self-imposed shackles that impede your journey.

Chapter 2

Nurturing a Mindset of Progress

Fostering a mindset of growth plays a pivotal role in realizing our objectives and unveiling our inherent brilliance. A growth mindset revolves around the conviction that our abilities and intellect can evolve through persistent effort, determination, and gleaning insights from our mistakes. In contrast, a fixed mindset adheres to the belief that our capabilities and intelligence are predetermined and immutable.

Delving into the narratives of various individuals who cultivated a growth mindset offers valuable insights into how we can foster this potent outlook within ourselves.

The Odyssey of Alex Chen

One prime illustration is Alex Chen, an aspiring artist. Early on, Alex held onto the notion that artistic talent was either innate or absent. However, Alex's journey took a turn when an art teacher guided him to view challenges as stepping stones rather than stumbling blocks. This shift in perspective allowed Alex to embrace experimentation and mistakes, fostering a growth mindset that propelled him toward mastery.

Emily Rodriguez's Journey

Another exemplar is Emily Rodriguez, a budding scientist. Initially, Emily subscribed to the belief that scientific aptitude was fixed and genetically determined. Yet, as she engaged in scientific inquiries, she encountered challenges that tested her convictions. Through mentorship and self-reflection, Emily learned to view setbacks as opportunities for improvement. This perspective shift, coupled with relentless determination, enabled her to cultivate a growth mindset and excel in her scientific pursuits.

The Contribution of Dr. Patel

Dr. Patel's narrative also stands as a testament to cultivating a growth mindset. Dr. Patel, an accomplished physician, initially confronted doubts regarding her proficiency in diagnosing complex cases. With the guidance of a mentor, Dr. Patel adopted a mindset that positioned errors as learning tools. This shift allowed her to embrace challenges and eventually establish herself as a proficient diagnostician.

Practical Strategies to Foster a Growth Mindset

- **Embrace Challenges**

Instead of evading challenges, welcome them as opportunities for expansion. When confronted with a demanding task, consider it a chance to cultivate fresh skills and understanding.

- **Embrace Risks**

Cast aside fear and venture into uncharted territory. Failures are integral to the learning journey, and taking risks can unveil novel avenues for growth and accomplishment.

- **Mistakes as Stepping Stones**

Rather than succumbing to discouragement, view mistakes as avenues for learning and refinement. Scrutinize errors to pinpoint areas that warrant improvement and devise novel strategies for success.

- **Engage in Self-Reflection**

Dedicate time for introspection, gauging your advancement and identifying areas ripe for enhancement. Leverage feedback as a tool for development, concentrating on avenues for improvement rather than dwelling on missteps.

- **Foster Positivity**

Cultivate a positive outlook and unearth silver linings in every scenario. This mindset fuels motivation and concentration on objectives.

- **Seek Learning from Others**

Access mentors and role models for guidance and support. Draw wisdom from their experiences and employ their insights in your own journey.

- **Nurture Persistence**

The essence of a growth mindset lies in perseverance. When confronted with obstacles, forge ahead and persevere. Setbacks are an intrinsic facet of the learning trajectory.

- **Prioritize the Process**

Rather than fixating solely on the end outcome, emphasize the journey of learning and advancement. Commemorate progress and small triumphs along the way.

- **Instill the Love of Learning**

The roots of a growth mindset lie in a passion for learning. Seek novel experiences and avenues for learning, approaching them with an open and inquisitive mindset.

In summation, the journey to fostering a growth mindset is a cornerstone in our quest to attain aspirations and tap into our concealed brilliance. The accounts of diverse figures such as Dr. Patel, Alex Chen, and Emily Rodriguez underline the potency of such a mindset in surmounting challenges and attaining greatness. By embracing challenges, redefining mistakes as learning tools, practicing persistence, and kindling a fervor for learning, we can cultivate a growth mindset and realize our utmost potential.

Chapter 3

Harnessing Inner Resilience and Determination

Accessing our inner reservoir of vigor and determination is pivotal to surmounting challenges and realizing triumph. This wellspring, characterized by unwavering energy and resolve, lies within us, providing the strength to navigate through adversity and attain our objectives. When we draw upon this inner strength, we gain access to a profound reservoir of resilience and bravery that empowers us to persevere through the most daunting circumstances. However, unearthing this inner potency is not always straightforward; it necessitates a resilient mindset and a willingness to venture beyond our comfort zones.

Testimonies of Empowerment through Inner Strength

An illustrative example of an individual who harnessed their inner power and determination is Amir Khan, a renowned athlete. Amir's journey was marked by numerous setbacks, including injuries and defeats. Rather than succumb to discouragement, he tapped into his inner strength and unwavering determination. With diligent effort and an indomitable spirit, he persevered through challenges, ultimately realizing victory and triumph in his sporting career.

Another embodiment of harnessing inner strength is Maya Patel, a dedicated educator. Maya faced resource constraints and resistance when she sought to establish an educational program for underprivileged children. Unfazed by these challenges, she channeled her inner resilience and determination, surmounting obstacles and successfully launching the program. Maya's unwavering commitment and resourcefulness stand as a testament to the potential within us to overcome hurdles.

Lucas Martinez, a passionate environmentalist, serves as yet another exemplar. In his pursuit to conserve natural habitats, Lucas confronted skepticism and bureaucracy. By tapping into his inner power and resolve, he weathered opposition and tirelessly advocated for environmental preservation. His enduring efforts showcase the transformative impact of harnessing inner strength.

Effective Strategies to Cultivate Inner Strength:

Establish Objectives: Setting clear goals instills a sense of purpose and direction. When objectives are defined, the motivation to draw upon inner strength to accomplish them is amplified.

Foster Self-Belief: Self-assurance in our capabilities is pivotal for accessing inner strength. When we harbor faith in our capacity to achieve, we are more inclined to transcend our limitations.

Learn from Adversity: Rather than perceiving challenges as setbacks, interpret them as chances for growth and learning. Each obstacle overcome bolsters inner strength and resilience.

Prioritize Self-Care: Nurturing our physical, emotional, and mental well-being is essential to accessing inner strength. Adequate sleep, a balanced diet, and engaging in activities that bring joy contribute to our reservoir of vigor.

Take Decisive Action: Taking proactive steps is a potent approach to tapping into inner strength. Each action taken reaffirms our capabilities and propels us toward success.

By tapping into our inner strength, we can forge a path to achievement and lead our most fulfilling lives. The stories of individuals like Amir Khan and Maya Patel underscore the possibility of surmounting adversity and leveraging inner power to attain remarkable feats. Through practicing self-care, setting goals, cultivating self-belief, and taking action, we can tap into our inner strength and unlock our boundless potential.

Chapter 4

Illuminating Purpose and Igniting Passion

Purpose and passion, often mentioned in the same breath, bear separate yet interconnected meanings. Purpose pertains to the fundamental reason for one's existence or the overarching objective that propels life's trajectory. Conversely, passion embodies intense enthusiasm and delight in an endeavor. The adage that discovering purpose and embracing passion can culminate in a meaningful and gratifying existence holds true.

Delving into the Uniqueness of Purpose

Purpose, the cornerstone of one's journey, requires introspection into what holds significance and the desired life accomplishments. Reflecting on values, strengths, and aspirations is beneficial. Queries like the following can aid in this pursuit:

- How can I contribute to the world?

- What talents and skills set me apart?

- What legacy do I yearn to leave?

- What would truly fulfill me in life?

As responses materialize, the path to uncovering one's purpose takes shape. This purpose may manifest as a grand global mission or a personal aspiration, such as being a nurturing parent. Regardless, it should evoke inspiration and motivation.

Untangling the Threads of Passion:

Discovering passion often proves more straightforward. Ponder activities that stir vitality, the ones that engross you for hours on end. This passion may express itself in creative outlets like writing or painting or in active pursuits like running or dancing. It might even be a curiosity yet to be explored.

Embarking on the Path of Pursuit:

Upon identifying purpose and passion, the subsequent step involves actively pursuing them. Here are a few practical exemplifications:

• For those driven to influence the world, volunteering for a cherished cause or choosing a profession aligned with personal values is viable.

• Should writing be the passion, commencing a blog or journaling offers an avenue for honing skills and sharing insights. Participating in writing classes or joining a writer's group can amplify craftsmanship.

• When the purpose is exceptional parenting, prioritizing robust connections with offspring and engaging in their lives takes precedence. Reading parenting literature or attending workshops enhances parenting proficiency.

• In the case of a fervor for running, setting a goal like a 5k or marathon and commencing training is a step forward. Joining a running club or securing a workout partner bolsters motivation.

Recounting Real-Life Narratives of Purpose:

A Tribute to Jane Goodall

Jane Goodall, the eminent primatologist, dedicated her life to studying chimpanzees and advocating for their safeguarding. Her affinity for animals and aspiration to make a positive impact impelled her to undertake this mission, rendering her a beacon in conservation efforts.

The Visionary Elon Musk

The billionaire entrepreneur, Elon Musk, founded prosperous companies such as Tesla and SpaceX, driven by a purpose to expedite the transition to sustainable energy and establish humanity as a multi-planetary species. His relentless commitment and progress toward these ambitions spotlight his purpose-driven journey.

The Marvel of Jack Andraka

Jack Andraka, a prodigious inventor, crafted a groundbreaking pancreatic cancer test at a tender age of 15. His ardor for science and resolve to effect change fueled this endeavor, propelling him into the vanguard of the fight against cancer.

These exemplars unravel how purpose, passion, and perseverance intertwine. Guided by introspection and zeal, these individuals translated their aspirations into tangible achievements, inspiring others to embark on their own purpose-driven odysseys.

In conclusion, unearthing purpose and igniting passion necessitates time and self-discovery. This journey is an amalgamation of self-reflection and an expedition through pursuits that invigorate the spirit. As you embark on this journey, allow patience to be your ally and let the pursuit of inspiration and motivation guide your course. Just as the stories of individuals like Jane Goodall, Elon Musk, and

Jack Andraka show, a life driven by purpose and kindled by passion has the potential to leave an indelible mark on the world, serving as an enduring source of inspiration and transformation.

Chapter 5

Crafting a Vision for Your Life: Blueprint for Achievement

A life vision serves as a compass guiding us toward our aspirations and potential. Without this compass, the journey becomes disoriented, making it challenging to discern where our efforts should be directed and how progress can be made toward our desired outcomes. Within this chapter, we delve into the art of creating a life vision, illustrating the process through the transformative narratives of accomplished individuals who have forged their own paths.

Unveiling the Tapestry of a Life Vision

A life vision is a vivid and captivating portrayal of the future we desire. It encompasses our values, priorities, and goals, intricately woven to outline what we aim to achieve in our personal and professional spheres. Aspirational, inspiring, and motivating, a life vision mirrors our deepest yearnings, serving as a roadmap to manifest these yearnings into reality.

Forging the Path to a Life Vision

Crafting a life vision necessitates introspection and reflection. It involves plumbing the depths of our desires, values, and purpose. The journey to creating a life vision unfolds in these steps:

- Reflect on Your Values and Priorities:

The initial stride in creating a life vision is to ponder your values and priorities. What holds paramount significance to you? What ranks above all else? What are your enduring ambitions? Reflecting on these queries assists in refining your values and priorities and charting the trajectory of your life's journey.

- Unearth Your Strengths and Passions:

Subsequently, unearth your strengths and passions. What are your proficiencies? What activities invigorate you? What flows naturally from your being? Identifying your strengths and passions enables their integration into your life vision, harnessing them to advance toward your goals.

- Forge Specific Goals:

With a clear grasp of your values, priorities, strengths, and passions, it's time to shape specific goals. Employ the SMART principle: Specific, Measurable, Achievable, Relevant, and Time-bound. Precise goals galvanize your efforts, charting a definitive course toward your life vision.

- Craft an Action Blueprint:

Post-establishing your goals, the next step entails crafting a comprehensive action blueprint. This blueprint delineates the precise steps required to realize your goals, complete with timelines, milestones, and deadlines. It serves as a navigational guide, aiding in monitoring progress and maintaining alignment with your life vision.

Illustrating the Path with Real-Life Narratives

To elucidate the life vision creation process, let's immerse ourselves in the journeys of three individuals who've etched their life visions into reality:

- *Dr. Maya Patel*

Dr. Maya Patel envisioned a world where healthcare was accessible to all, regardless of their socio-economic status. Her pursuit led her to establish mobile clinics that provide medical care to underserved communities. Through her unwavering dedication, she is creating a positive impact on the health and lives of countless individuals.

- *Samir Khan*

Samir Khan, an avid environmentalist, envisioned a future where renewable energy sources were harnessed to combat climate change. Inspired by this vision, he co-founded a startup that develops innovative solar technologies. His commitment and innovation are contributing to a greener and more sustainable world.

- *Elena Rodriguez*

Elena Rodriguez's life vision revolved around empowering underprivileged youth through education. She founded a non-profit organization that offers scholarships and mentorship programs to disadvantaged students. Through her tireless efforts, she is helping these students break the cycle of poverty and achieve their dreams.

Creating a life vision is an odyssey of self-discovery and aspiration. It demands patience, introspection, and dedication. Just as the stories of Dr. Maya Patel, Samir Khan, and Elena Rodriguez exemplify, a well-crafted life vision can surmount challenges and fuel extraordinary achievements. By discerning your aspirations and why they resonate with you, your focus and determination remain unswerving, even when confronted with obstacles. As you journey toward your life vision, remember that it's a compass guiding you toward a life enriched with purpose, fulfillment, and the realization of your true potential.

Chapter 6

Navigating the Path of Meaningful Goal Setting and Achievement

Setting and achieving meaningful goals lays the cornerstone for a fulfilling and purposeful life. Goals serve as beacons, illuminating the direction to our aspirations, bolstering our focus, and igniting the fire of motivation within us. Yet, the journey to realizing our goals entails more than just their establishment; it demands resolute action and a steadfast commitment to their attainment. In this chapter, we embark on an exploration of the art and science behind setting and achieving meaningful goals. Practical examples will guide us through each step of this transformative journey.

- **Embracing the Essence of Values and Priorities:**

Crafting meaningful goals commences with a keen understanding of your values and priorities. Unveiling what resonates most deeply with you is pivotal in ensuring your goals align harmoniously with your true essence. Imagine valuing health and wellness; your goal might revolve around adopting a consistent exercise routine and a balanced diet.

- **Paving the Way for SMART Goals:**

Once you've delved into your values and priorities, it's time to fashion your goals. To imbue your goals with effectiveness, they must adhere to the SMART framework: Specific, Measurable, Achievable, Relevant, and Time-bound. Instead of a vague aspiration to "get fit," your SMART goal might read as "shed 10 pounds in 3 months by engaging in thrice-weekly exercise and embracing a nourishing diet."

- **Unwrapping the Power of Incremental Goals:**

Conquering monumental goals is facilitated by disassembling them into bite-sized, attainable portions. This strategy thwarts overwhelm and bolsters motivation by celebrating progress along the way. Visualize your overarching goal of establishing a successful business; breaking it down entails crafting sub-goals like market research, business plan formulation, and funding procurement.

Concretizing Aspirations through Writing:

Transcribing your goals onto paper endows them with tangibility and clarity. It encourages deeper contemplation and the formulation of a meticulous plan for goal attainment, accompanied by a progress-tracking mechanism.

- **Creating a Blueprint of Action:**

As your goals take shape, an action blueprint comes into play. This blueprint outlines each step essential in navigating toward your aspirations. Creating this blueprint fosters organization and concentration, ensuring steady strides toward realizing your goals. Imagine aspiring to run a marathon; your action plan might encompass selecting a training program, procuring suitable running gear, and scheduling runs.

- **Measuring the Path of Progress:**

Regular progress tracking safeguards you against veering off course. Consistently evaluating your advancement sustains motivation and unveils areas warranting adjustment. Ponder a goal to amass $10,000 in a year; tracking your progress entails periodic assessment of your bank account and financial adjustments if needed.

- **Harnessing the Power of Accountability:**

Sharing your goals with others and soliciting their support can wield remarkable accountability. Establishing mechanisms like journal tracking or partnering with a coach or mentor empowers you to maintain steadfast focus.

- **Celebrating Triumphs along the Path:**

Triumphing over goals is an accomplishment deserving of celebration. Marking milestones fuels motivation and acknowledges your perseverance and progress. Envision a goal of mastering a new language; celebrating might involve planning a trip to a locale where the language is spoken and practicing your newfound skills.

- **Learning from Stumbles and Shortcomings:**

Viewing failures as stepping stones to success is fundamental. Gleaning insights from setbacks paves the way for course correction and future triumphs. Picture aspiring to complete a marathon but falling short; reflection might prompt adjustments in your training regimen, dietary habits, and guidance from experienced runners.

Unfurling the Banner of Flexibility and Adaptability:

Journeying toward your goals necessitates a pliable disposition, as life often ushers in unexpected turns. Flexibility empowers progress despite adversity. Imagine aiming to complete a half-marathon in six months; while your initial training regimen may prove unfeasible due to unforeseen circumstances, embracing a different training program or adopting cross-training can facilitate the continuation of your journey.

The expedition of setting and achieving meaningful goals orchestrates a symphony of intention, action, and adaptation. It beckons us to delve into our values, construct SMART goals, chart progress, celebrate victories, and learn from setbacks. Remaining adaptable in the face of life's fluctuations, like a captain adjusting their sails to navigate unforeseen currents, ensures a trajectory steadfastly aligned with our aspirations. Each step of the journey enriches our tapestry of life with purpose, achievement, and growth.

Chapter 7

Nurturing Your Well-Being and Growth in Today's Fast-Paced World

Navigating the Maze of Self-Care and Personal Development:

In the relentless rhythm of modern existence, the clamor of responsibilities often drowns out the whispers of self-care and personal growth. The pursuit of careers, relationships, and obligations sometimes eclipses the essential practice of tending to our own well-being. This results in burnout and a pervasive sense of hollowness.

Yet, embracing self-care and personal development is not only a solace for the soul but a compass for a thriving, harmonious life. This chapter delves into the significance of self-care and personal development and offers concrete examples of how to anchor these practices in your daily journey.

Unwrapping the Layers of Self-Care and Personal Development:

Self-care involves nurturing your physical, mental, and emotional facets. Activities like meditation, exercise, journaling, or cherishing moments with loved ones infuse vitality into these dimensions. Personal development, in contrast, centers around the evolution of various aspects of your life, be it your career, relationships, or inner growth. The symbiotic interplay of self-care and personal development weaves a tapestry of fulfillment and goal actualization.

The Art of Prioritizing Self-Care and Personal Development:

Carving out time for self-care and personal development must become a non-negotiable in your life. Allocate dedicated moments daily or weekly to engage in these enriching pursuits. Imagine penciling in a weekly yoga class or setting aside an hour each night to immerse yourself in a personal development book. The consistency of these practices amplifies their transformative power.

Elevating Self-Care and Personal Development through Intention:

Harness the potency of intention by aligning self-care and personal development with your authentic aspirations. Reflect on what evokes joy, what activities resonate profoundly, and which areas of your life beckon for refinement. This discernment births a plan to seamlessly integrate these endeavors into your daily or weekly routine.

Building Boundaries: The Keystone to Prioritization:

Establishing boundaries serves as the cornerstone of prioritizing self-care and personal development. Uttering a decisive "no" to commitments misaligned with your values and momentarily disconnecting from energy-draining pursuits replenishes your reserves for rejuvenating activities.

The Tapestry of Improved Well-Being:

Engaging in self-care and personal development intricately weaves a tapestry of enriched well-being. Physical exercise endows vitality, meditation alleviates stress, and personal growth augments self-esteem. The amalgamation of these practices bestows upon you a heightened quality of life.

A Lighthouse for Overall Success:

Prioritizing self-care and personal development radiates an aura of success into every facet of your existence. Nurturing your well-being and honing your skills equips you to surmount obstacles and manifest aspirations. If, for instance, you prioritize sleep and exercise as part of your self-care regimen, your amplified energy and laser-like focus will empower you to triumph over your work or creative projects.

Seeking Allies on the Path:

Augmenting your pursuit of self-care and personal development through alliances with others amplifies your journey. Seek the support of mentors, friends, or coaches; these allies catalyze your growth by their presence, encouragement, and wisdom.

A Mindset Revolution: Unveiling the Necessity of Self-Care and Personal Development:

The transformation of prioritizing self-care and personal development necessitates a paradigm shift. Dispelling the notion that self-care is selfish or that personal growth is an endeavor of convenience is fundamental. These practices affirm that nurturing oneself is an act of reverence, and personal evolution is a lifelong journey of purpose and dedication.

In a nutshell, the elevation of self-care and personal development isn't just an indulgence; it's a testament to your commitment to living a life brimming with happiness, health, and fulfillment. Embrace moments for self-care, erect boundaries, and absorb wisdom from others. Cultivate self-care and personal development as essential foundations for living your most vibrant, flourishing life.

Chapter 8

Nurturing Positivity and Growth Mindsets for a Flourishing Life

The cultivation of positive habits and mindsets serves as a compass guiding individuals toward a life imbued with fulfillment and triumph. In the fabric of these habits and mindsets lies the key to embracing challenges with optimism and fostering personal development. This chapter embarks on a journey through ten practical strategies that illuminate the path to nurturing positive habits and mindsets, breathing vitality and contentment into every facet of existence.

- **Embracing Gratitude:**

Gratitude stands as a beacon of positivity, allowing us to appreciate the blessings in our lives. By cultivating gratitude, we pivot from dwelling on shortcomings to celebrating our abundance. A gratitude journal or heartfelt expressions of appreciation serve as nurturing grounds for this practice.

- **Infusing Growth Mindsets:**

The growth mindset is a cornerstone of progress, fueling the belief that effort can enhance skills and intelligence. It encourages the embrace of challenges as stepping stones to advancement. To foster a growth mindset, invest in the process of learning and seek feedback as a stepping stone to refinement.

- **Crafting Positive Intentions:**

AWAKENING YOUR INNER EXCELLENCE: MASTERING YOUR MIND FOR A FULFILLING LIFE

The crafting of positive intentions instills purpose and direction into our daily endeavors. By delineating clear intentions for days, weeks, or months, we instill a forward-looking momentum. Translating these intentions into written goals fortifies their impact.

- **Elevating Self-Care Rituals:**

Self-care emerges as the nurturing bedrock of positive habits and mindsets. It necessitates the tender nurturing of our physical, emotional, and mental realms. Partake in activities that rejuvenate the spirit and foster tranquility, while carving out time for rest.

- **Penetrating Mindful Reflection:**

Mindful reflection is a sanctuary for self-discovery, fostering an unclouded comprehension of our thoughts and emotions. By setting aside a mindful moment each day, we kindle self-awareness, paving the way for growth and mindful living.

- **Cultivating a Garden of Positive Habits:**

Positive habits constitute the seeds of success. To cultivate them, dissect life into realms that require nurturing. Subsequently, set achievable goals that spring from these realms. For instance, embarking on a 30-minute daily exercise routine fosters positive change in physical well-being.

- **Orbiting in a Positive Atmosphere:**

The orbit we traverse in the company of others can dramatically influence our mindset. Envelop yourself in the embrace of individuals radiating positivity and support. This constellation of allies, ranging from friends to mentors, fuels growth and emboldens your journey.

- **Embracing Failure as a Stepping Stone:**

Embracing failure as a bridge to growth is a transformative mindset. Through the lens of such a perspective, setbacks become portals to learning and refinement. Reflect on your experiences, extracting lessons that feed your growth.

- **The Art of Morning Rituals**:

Morning rituals orchestrate the symphony of each day, shaping its tone and resonance. Develop morning habits that envelop your day in positivity, whether it's exercise, meditation, or introspective journaling.

- **Cultivating Self-Compassion:**

The cultivation of self-compassion is a tribute to our humanity. When confronted with setbacks or challenges, tenderly guide yourself with self-talk that soothes rather than criticizes. Acknowledge that these tribulations are integral to the journey of evolution.

A Glimpse into the Life of Lucy:

AWAKENING YOUR INNER EXCELLENCE: MASTERING YOUR MIND FOR A FULFILLING LIFE

Enter Lucy, a vivacious woman who grappled with pessimism and a stagnating mindset. These shackles tethered her to negativity, stifling her growth and halting her journey toward success. However, Lucy embarked on a transformational expedition that altered her course.

Lucy embarked on a journey of cultivating positive habits and mindsets. She initiated with baby steps, setting attainable goals that harmonized with her values. Lucy practiced gratitude by journaling daily blessings, embarking on a transformative journey from a realm of scarcity to one of abundance.

She sought refuge in a growth mindset, reframing challenges as opportunities for development. This newfound mindset catapulted her forward, overcoming obstacles with grace. Lucy diligently set intentions for each day, anchoring herself in a sense of purpose and determination.

Lucy embraced self-care rituals, cherishing moments of reprieve and cultivating habits that recharged her spirit. Surrounding herself with optimistic souls breathed life into her journey, while the acceptance of failure as a stepping stone provided her with renewed vigor.

Through her diligent morning rituals, Lucy kindled a daily fire of positivity, greeting each day with fervor and zest. Armed with self-compassion, she navigated failures with a gentle understanding, using them as catalysts for growth.

In summary, the journey of cultivating positive habits and mindsets metamorphosed Lucy's existence. This transformation fortified her spirit, catalyzed her growth, and ignited her pursuit of a more fulfilling life.

In a nutshell, the cultivation of positive habits and mindsets is an indispensable gateway to a life adorned with fulfillment and accomplishment.

Chapter 9

Weaving Bonds of Connection and Camaraderie

Within the intricate tapestry of existence, forging robust relationships and connections emerges as a quintessential thread, vitalizing a life brimming with fulfillment. As social beings, the connections we nurture with others are the very essence that propels us forward. Yet, constructing profound relationships demands time, endeavor, and a willingness to embrace vulnerability. This chapter navigates through a constellation of strategies that illuminate the pathway toward cultivating sturdy relationships and connections, illustrated through vivid narratives.

- **Embarking with Attentive Listening**

The cornerstone of potent relationships lies in the art of active listening. Herein, the act of truly comprehending another's words, devoid of judgment or interruption, bridges the gap between hearts. This dynamic cultivates trust and comprehension, exemplified when Emily leaned in to listen and empathize with her friend's struggles, thereby nurturing a resilient friendship.

- **Presence: A Gift in the Moment**

The essence of connection blooms when we offer the gift of our presence. This entails relinquishing distractions, locking eyes, and bestowing genuine interest upon the speaker. A testament to value is etched through this act, as Alex, upon meeting his partner's parents, offered undivided attention, fostering an unbreakable connection.

- **Seeds of Gratitude and Appreciation**

The petals of robust relationships unfurl when nurtured with gratitude and appreciation. In these small gestures, a world of significance is unveiled. Whether in the form of heartfelt thanks or thoughtful deeds, these acts bolster relationships. Jake's gesture of gratitude towards a coworker after their collaborative effort instilled a deeper bond.

- **Reliability and Trust: The Bedrock**

The architecture of sturdy relationships necessitates a foundation of trust and reliability. Upholding commitments, demonstrating dependability, and safeguarding confidences knit the fabric of trust. Tom's punctuality and dedication while assisting his friend in moving echoed a symphony of reliability, reinforcing their unshakable bond.

- **Vulnerability as the Glue**

The crucible for substantial relationships is vulnerability. Herein, the unveiling of thoughts, emotions, and experiences ignites the path to mutual understanding. This journey fosters profound bonds, as Sarah and her sister discovered when they navigated their differences, emerging with a renewed closeness.

- **The Thread of Shared Interests**

Common interests and shared experiences are the threads that weave strong relationships. As curiosity guides the exploration of one another's passions, connections burgeon. The tale of Tim's blossoming friendship with his gardening-loving neighbor epitomizes the magic of shared endeavors.

- **Forgiveness: A Portal to Growth**

Conflict, inevitable in the human tapestry, unveils the transformative power of forgiveness. Embracing these moments, characterized by vulnerability, solidifies connections. As Jane and her coworker chose dialogue over discord, their relationship transcended conflict, resurfacing stronger than ever.

- **Honoring Boundaries: A Gesture of Respect**

Respecting the boundaries of others is a testament to the valorization of relationships. Intuitive cues and attentiveness embody this respect. Dave's recognition of his friend's boundary and subsequent redirection of conversation portrays a reverent act, nurturing mutual esteem.

- **The Symphony of Empathy and Compassion:**

The threads of empathy and compassion weave intricate patterns in the tapestry of robust relationships. The practice of understanding another's perspective and extending a hand of support, especially in times of adversity, fosters enduring bonds. In the realm of Jane's corporate journey, empathy unveiled unity and collaboration.

A Glimpse into the Life of Lucas

AWAKENING YOUR INNER EXCELLENCE: MASTERING YOUR MIND FOR A FULFILLING LIFE

Meet Lucas, a soul who once wrestled with pessimism and stagnant connections. Shrouded in negativity, Lucas was stymied in his pursuit of authentic relationships. But the dawn of transformation beckoned, inspiring him to embark on an odyssey of connection.

Lucas embarked on the journey of cultivating robust relationships and connections. He initiated with earnest steps, setting aside judgments to truly understand others' stories. This sincere engagement propelled trust and understanding, breathing vitality into his bonds. The newfound connection with his colleague, forged through genuine listening, bore testimony to the magic of attentive engagement.

As he traversed the realm of connection, Lucas unveiled the beauty of presence. By shelving distractions and immersing himself in conversations, he breathed life into relationships. His encounter with his partner's parents unfurled this transformation, anchoring them in an authentic connection.

Lucas realized the potency of gratitude as he showered appreciation upon the significant figures in his life. Through thoughtful gestures and words, he nurtured bonds, leaving an indelible impact. His thanksgiving to a colleague post joint endeavors was a testament to this gesture.

The evolution of Lucas's connections was further propelled by vulnerability. Sharing his thoughts and emotions, while welcoming others' perspectives, etched deeper connections. As he opened up to his friend, their bond deepened, enveloping them in a web of mutual support.

Common interests also acted as the wind beneath Lucas's wings, as he explored shared passions with friends. He began to respect boundaries, honoring the uniqueness of each relationship. This newfound awareness, coupled with empathy and compassion, crafted connections that stood the test of time.

In essence, Lucas's voyage illuminated the art of building robust relationships and connections. From attentive listening to embracing vulnerability, his endeavors culminated in a tapestry woven with threads of authenticity and trust.

In summary, constructing sturdy relationships and connections is a symphony of presence, vulnerability, and compassion. Amidst the tendrils of human interaction, the essence of connection flourishes, be it in the workplace, friendships, or familial bonds. Through the cultivation of these connections, lives are enriched, and a tapestry of fulfillment is meticulously woven.

Chapter 10

Triumphing Over Trials with Unyielding Spirit and Determination

In the intricate mosaic of existence, the path is often dotted with obstacles and challenges that threaten to thwart our journey. Yet, in the resplendent tapestry of human resilience and indomitable grit, lies the ability to surmount these trials and emerge stronger, wiser, and more triumphant. This chapter delves into the essence of resilience and grit, weaving real-life narratives that bear witness to the awe-inspiring capacity of individuals to conquer adversity.

Resilience, akin to a phoenix rising from the ashes, encompasses the power to rebound from adversity and forge ahead with unwavering determination. Rooted in the tenacity to remain steadfast in the face of turmoil, it defies setbacks and refrains from allowing them to script our narrative. Bethany Hamilton's voyage epitomizes resilience's brilliance. Struck by a shark's ruthless attack at a tender age, Bethany's unyielding spirit refused to bow to fate. Rather, she persisted, channeling her dreams into conquering the waves, metamorphosing into an icon of resilience as she ascended to the zenith of female surfers.

On the parallel spectrum of endurance and aspiration, grit emerges as the virtuous fusion of passion and perseverance. Within its realm resides the audacity to keep our gaze fixed on distant horizons, navigating past impediments in relentless pursuit of our aspirations. In the annals of grit's testament stands Simone Biles, an Olympian adorned with unwavering grit and relentless determination. Through injuries and trials, she harnessed her resolve, etching her name among the pantheon of gymnastic legends.

The narrative of Colonel Harland Sanders unfurls as a living testament to the vitality of grit. Born into the crucible of hardship, his journey epitomizes the ardor to transcend limitations. Abandoning school for odd jobs, he found solace in the culinary realm. Possessing an ardent culinary passion, he donned the apron and endeavored to kindle his culinary fire. Through tribulations that would have shattered others, he emerged unfazed, his grit igniting a trail to the KFC empire, which now spans the globe.

Into the tapestry of this discourse steps forth Jessica, a tenacious young woman resolute in her pursuit of a medical career. Hindered by financial constraints and familial obligations, her aspirations seemed eclipsed by looming clouds. Yet, Jessica's story is one of resilience, as she navigated through these barriers with unfaltering spirit. Balancing part-time jobs, studies, and familial responsibilities, she illuminated the trail for others by embodying resilience's brilliance.

Concurrently, Joshua's tale resonates with the symphony of resilience and grit. Overcoming the shackles of adversity, Joshua harnessed his disability to inspire others. Born with visual impairment, he refused to let his limitations curtail his aspirations. Through a growth mindset, he cultivated the resilience to ascend each summit, dispelling doubts with his unyielding spirit.

Amidst the annals of inspiration, the account of Maya dances into view. Plunged into a vortex of despair following a career setback, she transformed her despair into the crucible of resilience. Her foray into self-discovery, guided by a growth mindset, saw her emerging from the abyss stronger and brimming with purpose. Maya's story illustrates that resilience is not just the ability to withstand adversity, but the means to metamorphose it into an opportunity for growth.

To cultivate resilience and grit, the canvas of our mindset must be adorned with the hues of growth. Within the tapestry of challenges, the lens of growth perceives opportunities for evolution and learning. In the saga of Nick Vujicic, the canvas illuminates this perspective. Born without limbs, Nick's growth mindset propelled him to transcend his physical constraints, employing his story as a beacon of inspiration to ignite the spirits of others.

Nurturing resilience and grit also hinges on grounding ourselves in the present. The allure of the future and echoes of the past often obscure the beauty of the present moment. The journey of Aron Ralston, encapsulated in his confinement within nature's grasp, underscores the essence of resilience. Amidst despair, his focus never wavered, his mind enveloped by the struggle for survival. His story imparts the wisdom that resilience blooms when nurtured within the confines of the present, regardless of external turmoil.

A glance towards the world of Elsa reveals the significance of a robust support network. Hailing from a tumultuous background, Elsa weathered storms through the unwavering support of friends and mentors. Her journey underscores the importance of a strong social fabric as a bolstering force, augmenting resilience and grit in the face of adversity.

Furthermore, the anatomy of resilience and grit accommodates adaptability. When the paths we tread transform, the ability to recalibrate our approach becomes essential. This essence materializes within Steve Jobs' narrative. Dethroned from his creation, he embraced adversity as an opportunity, birthing a phoenix from the ashes and leaving an indelible mark on the world.

Setbacks and failures, rather than shadows, are stepping stones to illumination in the landscape of resilience and grit. In their embrace, growth flourishes, nurturing the resilience to transcend challenges. The chronicles of Emma bear witness to this truth. Her initial business failure spurred her onto the path of self-discovery and learning, encapsulating the essence that the darkest moments harbor the potential for the most radiant transformations.

In the grand tapestry of existence, resilience and grit emerge as luminous threads, intertwining to form a mosaic of unyielding spirit and unrelenting determination. Through a growth mindset, present-centered focus, support networks, and adaptability, individuals can harness the formidable power of these traits to surmount the highest peaks and emerge victorious from life's valleys. Thus, the crucible of adversity becomes the forge for character, resilience, and the triumphant symphony of grit.

Chapter 11

Embracing a Mindset for Achieving Success

In the grand tapestry of life, weaving the threads of achievement requires a mindset that aligns with success. This mindset isn't a secret code, but rather a way of thinking and acting that propels individuals toward greatness. In this chapter, we embark on an expedition to uncover the secrets of cultivating a mindset primed for success, illuminating its facets through the prism of real-life stories.

Step into the world of Jack, a young entrepreneur driven by a fire of ambition. The first step in developing a success-oriented mindset is to look beyond the hurdles and see the potential in challenges. Those who rise above are not daunted by roadblocks, for they recognize that these are opportunities in disguise. When told that his idea for a revolutionary app was too bold, Jack didn't falter. Instead, he saw this skepticism as a chance to refine his vision and make it even more groundbreaking. This perspective, akin to a sculptor chiseling a masterpiece, is what laid the foundation for his app's massive success.

Equally significant is the dance of failure within this narrative. Unlike a dead-end, failure is a crossroads that invites exploration. Maria's story embodies this essence. When her initial business venture floundered, she wasn't shattered. Instead, she embraced the wisdom within Thomas Edison's words, "I have not failed. I've just found 10,000 ways that won't work." With each setback, she unraveled lessons that sculpted her journey to success, her determination fanning the flames of resilience.

And as we delve further, we stumble upon the treasure trove of calculated risks. Take a glimpse into the life of Ethan, an inventor who dared to tread where none had before. At the heart of a success-oriented mindset is the audacity to leap into the unknown, for those who do not risk cannot truly soar. Like the pioneer who forges uncharted territory, Ethan left the confines of the familiar to dive headfirst into his invention. His calculated risk, reminiscent of a trapeze artist mid-flight, led him to discoveries that revolutionized his field.

A key component of the success-oriented mindset is the melody of hard work and perseverance. Journey alongside Lily, a dedicated athlete on a quest for excellence. Success is not a fleeting affair; it emerges from the loom of time and effort. Just as a blacksmith hammers molten metal to forge steel, Lily's unyielding practice and steadfast resolve shaped her into a champion. In her story, we discover that the true elixir of success is the sweat of perseverance.

Venture into the realm of Samantha, an aspiring artist who discovered the magic of mentors. A crucial brick in the wall of success is surrounding oneself with those who elevate and inspire. Like a constellation guiding a ship, mentors and positive influences illuminate the path to achievement. Samantha's journey is adorned with the wisdom bestowed by her artistic guide, propelling her to new heights of creativity.

In the world of Julian, purpose and vision stand as beacons of a success-oriented mindset. A lighthouse guiding ships through tumultuous waters, purpose offers direction and meaning. Julian's story mirrors the tenacity of a mountaineer, ascending summits with unwavering resolve. His success is sculpted by his unwavering focus on his purpose, casting shadows upon the obstacles that tried to deter him.

A tapestry of adaptability interweaves within the narrative of Mia. In the ever-shifting sands of life, adaptability is the ship's sail, adjusting to changing winds. Those who pivot and adjust their strategies sail past storms with tenacity. Just as a tree bends with the wind but stands tall, Mia's agility sculpted her path, allowing her to circumvent obstacles and emerge triumphant.

A growth mindset unfurls within the chronicles of Luke, the thirst for knowledge like a lantern guiding his way. Success is not a static destination; it's a journey of perpetual learning. Just as a river gathers knowledge from the lands it traverses, Luke gathered wisdom from his experiences and inquisitions. His pursuit of knowledge, akin to a scholar in pursuit of hidden truths, propelled him to heights unimagined.

As we conclude this exploration, we encounter the story of Emily, a beacon of resilience amidst life's tempests. A success-oriented mindset is a shield against adversity, for those who rise after a fall are not defeated but transformed. Emily's journey, akin to a phoenix's rebirth from ashes, witnessed her emerge from adversity with newfound strength and determination.

In the intricate mosaic of life, a success-oriented mindset shines as the jewel in the crown of achievement. It's the compass guiding the explorers, the wings lifting the dreamers, and the anchor grounding the visionaries. Through opportunities seized, failure embraced, risks calculated, and purpose aligned, individuals foster a mindset that transforms aspirations into reality. As we venture forth with this newfound knowledge, we weave our own narratives of success, embodying the essence of greatness within every step we take.

Chapter 12

Embracing Change and Taking Bold Action for Personal Growth

Life is a canvas of constant change, a symphony of evolution that demands our participation. Yet, nestled within our comfort zones, we often resist the allure of transformation. Stagnation might feel cozy, but it's on the precipice of change that true growth dances. In this chapter, we embark on a journey to understand how to stretch our wings beyond the familiar, embracing the winds of change to fuel our personal growth.

The journey commences with a compass, a map to identify the areas yearning for our attention. The first step toward change is acknowledging where growth is beckoning us. We assess our careers, our relationships, and the vast landscapes of personal development. With clarity, we draw a roadmap that illuminates the path toward our goals. These goals, like beacons guiding sailors, must challenge us, nudging us out of our comfort zones while remaining within the realm of possibility.

A tale of transformation unfolds as we enter Sarah's world, a world where change was met with action. Sarah, a dreamer, was once a door-to-door fax machine salesperson. However, her dissatisfaction with the undergarment options available for women lit the spark of an idea. Unfazed by her lack of fashion experience, she embarked on a journey to create Spanx. Years of research and development led her to become the youngest self-made female billionaire. Sarah's story echoes the sentiment that change, when embraced and acted upon, can pave the way for unprecedented success.

Like a pendulum, fear and uncertainty often sway us away from change. Yet, change's beauty is in its mystery, its invitation to discover the uncharted. A shift in perspective can transform fear into exhilaration. The unknown becomes a playground of opportunity rather than a dark abyss. Maria's story resonates as she faced the choice of a job opportunity in New York City. Fear battled her desire for growth, but she chose to embrace change. Despite initial struggles, her bold step led to a flourishing personal and professional life.

Our journey then meanders through the groves of support and encouragement. Friends, family, and mentors stand as pillars, lifting us toward our aspirations. Their insight, like lanterns in the night, guides us. John's pursuit of fitness began with a simple question to a personal trainer friend. With guidance and support, he transformed from uncertainty to success. Friends and mentors not only offer expertise but also provide a safety net when change feels daunting.

As the chapter unfolds, it becomes evident that action is the foundation upon which change rests. In the face of challenges, setbacks, and discomfort, action propels us forward. The key is to acknowledge obstacles as stepping stones, not stumbling blocks. An archetype of resilience is Ryan, who, despite a chronic illness, redefined his relationship with hiking. His journey from adversity to inspiration showcases the power of action, even in the face of adversity.

In closing, the symphony of change crescendos, urging us to dance to its rhythm. Embracing change and taking bold action is the gateway to personal growth. Through setting goals, reframing fear, seeking support, and persisting in the face of adversity, we can stretch our wings, soar beyond our comfort zones, and unlock the doors to our own potential. In the grand theater of life, change is the spotlight that reveals our truest selves, beckoning us to step onto the stage of our own evolution.

CONCLUSION

To wrap things up, I've talked about many different things and given you practical ways to deal with problems, grow a positive attitude, build good habits, make strong relationships, face challenges with strength, and welcome changes while taking action.

We've used stories about real people to show these ideas in action, and how they've used them to do amazing things. By looking at their experiences and using these ideas in your life, you can also uncover your own amazing abilities and do your best.

Don't forget, this journey to greatness isn't a one-time thing, but a continuous process of getting better and growing. As you go forward, it's important to keep your focus, stay inspired, and stick to the things we've talked about in this book.

With the right attitude and tools, you can face any problem and achieve amazing things in every part of your life. So, I urge you to take the first step today and start unlocking the power of your mind to make your life the best it can be. Remember, the greatness you're looking for is already inside you. You just need to let it out!

Awakening Your Inner Excellence

www.ingramcontent.com/pod-product-compliance
Lightning Source LLC
LaVergne TN
LVHW021553160125
801479LV00008B/433